CHRONIC PAIN

Malia Nahinu

This book is dedicated to everyone who lives with chronic pain. Whether that is mental, spiritual, emotional, or physical.

CONTENTS

The Pain is Within

A Civil War:

It's hard to tell whether
My pain is of the heart
Of the mind
Or of the air
That I am breathing

An air of anger
Of lack of clarity
Cementing itself into my nerves
Ripping apart my muscles
Tightening my vessels
Deteriorating the very spine that gives me strength

It's hard to tell where this pain came from
If it's really sports
Or sadness pinching every nerve
Stopping me from being happy

There is a war inside my body
There is a civil war inside my being
My sanity speaks to my insanity
They have no closure
They live in curses and hexes
Fighting each other for peace or chaos
Wanting to control my fate
And my spirit sits on timeout
Crying out to the oceans
"free me!!"

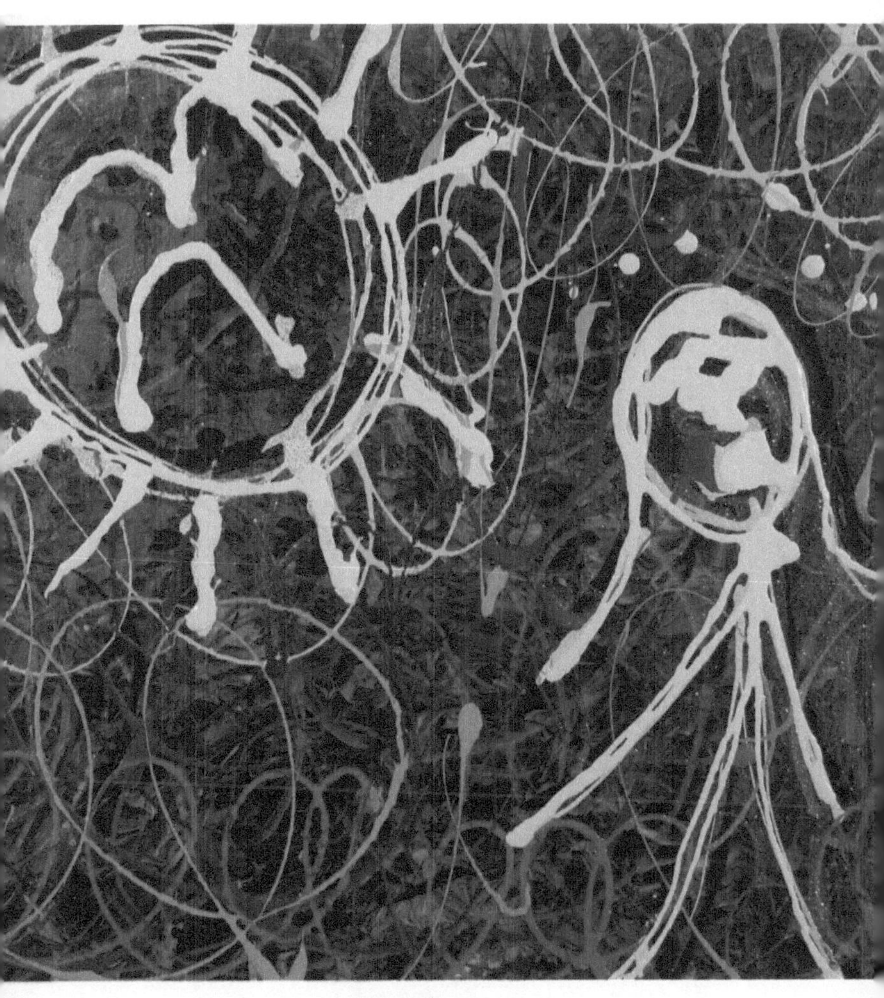

Sad Sad Sun

November 2019:

In November of 2019,
I received my MRI results on the train heading to
work
"You have disc degenerative, arthritic disease with a
cyst"
And I have to say,
With a cane, sitting in the Disability section since
September 2019,
I put my dark sunglasses on and held back my tears
as best as I could, but when I finally got to work, a
dear friend noticed right away
I've been living with intense back and sciatica pain
for two years at this point and hearing this news felt
devastating
It was as if I was being told that I would never
Have a normal life again, as if my life were normal…
I had been living in a cave through this pain, saying
no to dating, saying no to other activities and fun
events,
Isolating myself far before covid19 even came into
play,
I felt completely alone in my pain

* * *

And I held in this news for months before even
telling
anyone,
Except my mom, she knew, she told me I would get
through this,
And still to this day, I tend to not mention this detail
to anyone, because to be completely honest, I've
learned that people can't care about things they don't
relate to, and I don't expect people to relate to feeling
intense physical pain to the point of tears, to the point
of not leaving the house for a full day or two to rest,
just to be able to have enough energy to walk the next
five work days,
I don't expect anyone to relate to the level of
depression I have been feeling to the mild point of
suicidal thoughts, I don't expect anyone to relate to
that because they are not health professionals who've
been trained to help someone like me

The Mystical Palm Tree

Religious:

Everything changes when you're in physical pain
Every part of life I usually get irritated by
Or obsessed with that's usually out of my control
I just don't care about anymore
Everything suddenly turns into
"let me just get through this day and hope I can walk
tomorrow"
I sometimes even get religious
"Jesus Christ, why do I have to be in pain every
day!"

Wondering When it Ends

Rabbit Hole:

I can't tell where my pain exists
When I feel good
I feel happy
When I feel this burning numbness in my left leg
I feel depressed and angry
I can't tell if I am happy or just fed up with my life
I can't tell if I am just needing to eat healthier
Or if I should just give in and fall down the rabbit hole
Because I can't tell if this is the rabbit hole

The Crying Woman

• • •

Corn Chips:

Stinky man in sweats
Stinks of corn chips and farts
Smart phone and all
So, I don't feel bad for saying this
Hits me with his bike as he left
Shouting out sorry

Sort of a dim metaphor to the man I used to call hope

Only thing I can say now is thank you for the panic attacks
you gave me

The Crying Woman

Broken Pieces:

I think I am broken
Somewhere along the way
A piece of me was burnt, bruised, stolen
And I can't heal that part of me
I have tried so many remedies
From band aids to healthy foods, herbs, to music and
meditations
Lovers, validation and food
But there is nothing that makes me whole
No matter how hard I try
So, I find peace in the broken pieces
Hugging them, loving them
Understanding that without those pieces, I am me
And maybe, that means I am whole in the realization
that
I never needed to fix anything, that I am a broken
piece
Perfectly angled to fit into exactly what this god built
me for
Perfectly incomplete

Lost in Insanity

I'm Fine:

How do I stay angry at a sick person?
I can't
How do I rely on sickness?
I can't
At what point do recovered
addicts and alcoholics
start to really care for others
Start to really care about how I feel?
Instead of just caring about
having a guilt free conscious?
Maybe, they care too much,
Maybe, they have not embraced this part of
themselves
Because every time they have,
they were punished by liars and users,
Draining them of their love, leaving only toxic debris

I am always left wondering when these people will
let me in
Realizing maybe I am just not the right fit for their
lives

Did I free you with my forgiveness?
Do I set you free?
Please tell me I did
That's the least I can do
Since my heart knows no other way to be
But to care for you

Me?
I'm *fine*
- she say's

The Screaming Woman

Suffocation:

But,
If my heart can be honest
I feel caged in
Roped and tied down
Starved of what I felt was real
Realizing it was not
I feel suffocated
I can't breathe

She Couldn't Forget

Firefly Shift:

I'm in pain
An emotional heart attack
A mental fracture
Physically split with my legs and nerves up to the same
firefly shift
Inflamed and fired up for no reason
Lighting up the vulnerable parts of my veins
Weak muscles shouting at the tears in my eyes to hold on
for the ride
Another flare up

9 - 5

She Wonders:

My
Spine doesn't want to hold me up anymore
There's an old Lady in pink staring at me like
I don't deserve to sit in the disability section
I'm too young
Or perhaps my goddess energy is too much
To process
I explore this inside

How can she look fine on the outside?
But sit in the disability section?

\-   she wonders

My Native Ancestors Are Disappointed

1,2,3,4:

At what number do I tell myself enough is enough
1,2,3,4 emotionally unavailable men? More?
I'm not even sure what a strong man looks like
Or feels like energetically
How does he smile?
How does he respond?
How does he feel pain, or sadness, or happiness or
frustrations?
How does he show me he cares?
How does he work?
How does he react to my wall of stoic behaviors?
To my madness?
To my R O G U E Woman tendencies?
To my wild woman heart?

He Stripped Her Naked and Left Her Numb

Inner Child:

I'm all over the place
A splattered heart across the cement of my statuesque body
Once more
Chronic pain affects my eyes
And I can't find my third one at the moment
So, I can't see what's in front of me
I don't perceive the child within me
Who screams out for validation
Who just wants to be acknowledged
Who just wants to be hugged
Who just wants to feel loved

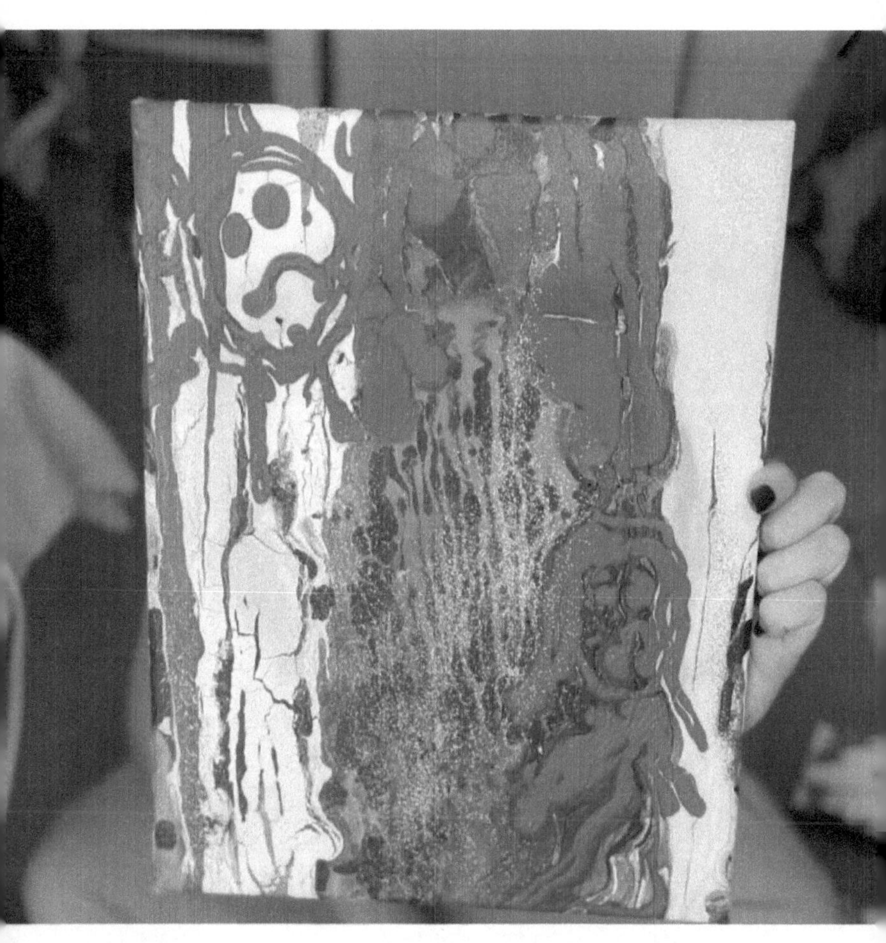

They Watch Your Sadness

Oceans:

I feel anger
It's deep
It feels like fire
Perhaps that is why
My body ravishes me so
To the oceans I seek
To the peace I believe in
Where shall I find you again?
The kind of happiness that comes and goes
It's like people really don't want me to find my home
They'd rather me be in poverty
Because that is the norm
To continue to appease a system built for my failure
But I don't believe this is true
I can see the one percent chance of me succeeding
So, I hold onto this cloud of hope
Despite my own faults yelling at me to give up
Despite my own depression trying to latch me to my sheets
Despite my own reservations to mediocrity
I desire to succeed

The Woman Who Haunted the Inner Child

Bulimia:

I suffered from bulimia
For seven years
I don't tell people this fact about my past
I think it scares them
I think it triggers people to realize
So many of us could be suffering right in front of us
With the very food we are supposed to see as fuel
No one noticed I was suffering until I told them
And still no one really cared
So, I shut up about it
Because I didn't have enough strength
to see myself inflicted with a disease
Until it ruined my twenties

I remember a time when I stared at my red eyes and puffy
face
In the mirror after throwing up three times in a row
Thinking to myself, "I should kill myself because this isn't
living"
I think it was in moments like those
Because it happened so often
That I realized I had to beat the odds
I had to overcome this
So, I can stand up one day and share this
Because I didn't have a therapist
I couldn't afford one
And I didn't have any friends because I held a secret, this
idea that I hated myself, that I didn't deserve love or

friends because of false words placed over my young
mind, because of a neglectful parent, because of
traumatizing collegiate events, because of this fake idea
that I was not good enough
The only way I beat the odds
Is by remembering those moments where I snuck into the
bathroom
To throw up
With the shower on to hide the noise
I think back and I remind myself how far I've come
That helps me get through the
habitual temptations that have
imbed into my mind

Psychedelic Imagination:

It's ironic
All these people wanting to be sober
And I exist in a space of drunk imagination
and terrible fantasies of weed and psychedelics
I wonder if they know my darkness
I wonder if that's why they keep coming back to me
It's like magnets
Our souls I mean
It's sick
It's toxic
It's passion

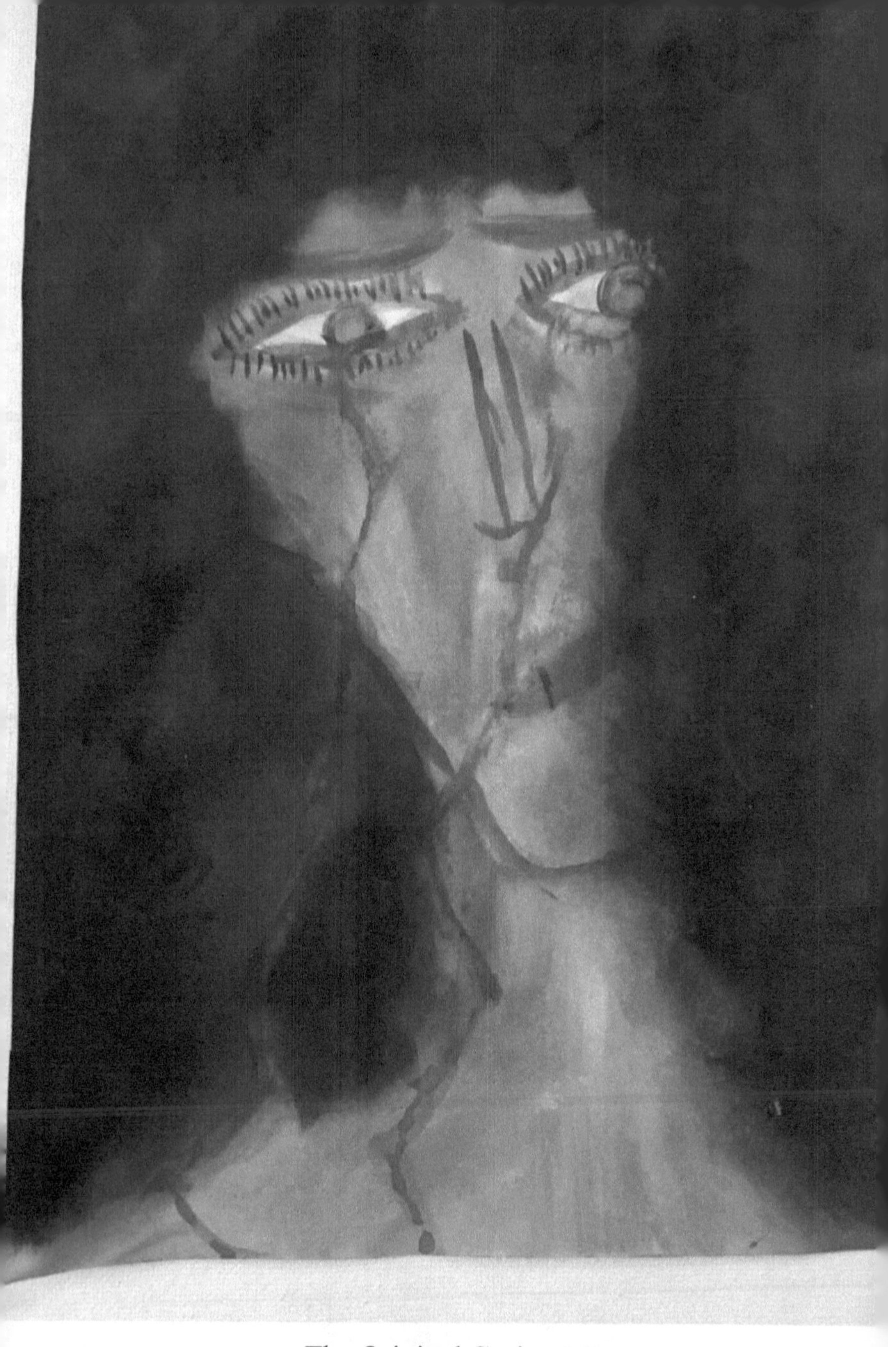

The Original Crying Man

Forget Forgiveness:

I accept forgiveness
But I don't forget easily
It's like a deep scar
A wound that pusses up whenever I remember these
people I've loved
And never would say these things to
Or do the things they've done to me to them
And I remember this each time a little harder
Every-time they mess up and come back to me like I'm
some sort of alter they pray to
Like I'm some sort of religion
they need saving
They need acceptance
They need warm femininity
A mother's heart
A woman's love
So desperate for it
They come to me as if I am the definition of sanctity
Like I'm some sort of divine feminine saint mary
But I'm not
I'm just like them
I'm pitiful and disrespectful
I have hate in my heart
And I feel nothing most of the tine
I'm annoyed by these things
By my own need to feel needed
By my own desire to love the unlovable
By my own passion for hope

She Waited for You

Haunted:

I don't tell anyone
But I'm always nervous when I'm walking around the Bay
Area
When I get on the trains
I'm terrified I'm going to see my dad one day
I'm horrified inside because there's a space he filled with
guilt
Like I'm supposed to care for him
For this man that never cared for me
So, when people ask me about my dad
I don't want to tell them anything
I don't have daddy issues
I have a lack of emotion towards his wellbeing
And this brings me peace
Until adult children with great parents ask me why…

The Man and His Past

The Cane of Empowerment:

This is the reality of my existence
How do I find empowerment with a cane?
With legs that feel like they should be stretched and
massaged every other hour?
How do I stand tall as powerful woman?
Confident woman
When I feel so tired?
When I remember how I gave my soul to a sport that stole
my 20's from me?
How do I express this to people who care about me?
I don't
I sit and I type on this computer
All the things I feel just to pretend I have an audience
Just to get through another train ride of people
Trying to invade the bubble of protection I imagined
around me
Not sure it actually works
But I still do it

Doodles

42

Panic Attacks:

Panic attack on the train
Fell in love with a figment
A fragment
A face in the wall
I mean it was never real
Never there
Couldn't tell me it cared
I was bare
Naked
Chest and all
Heart and everything
Ready for the fall
Crashing by myself into the ground

The Monster in the Mirror

Paranoia:

45

there is nothing more entertaining than staring at strangers
on a train
Especially young giant women in black sunglasses
In the disability section
At least that's what my paranoia says to me

The Universe in His Eyes

Please Don't:

I don't want my darkness dimmed
I don't want my lightness abused

Social Media is Fake

Clueless:

Screaming
Tears
Screaming
More tears
Irritation
Yelling
At the walls
At the bed
At the chairs
At the blank pages in front of me
At the Bobby pins on the floor
At the sun shining through the dirty, dusty shaded window
At my knees that keep hitting the desk
I hate everything
I hate people
I hate my family who doesn't check up on my sanity
I hate my friends who go on with their lives after I tell
them I'm suffering from this
I hate them because I wish I could feel free again
I hate them because I need them to call and they won't
hear my heart pleading for a friend that cares
There's no one here but me
And I can't take this reality

I'm falling down an endless sky
Into oblivion and no one notices
My roommate bangs on my door
Telling me to shut up
Telling me people outside will think I'm crazy
I think I am crazy
Maybe I should check myself in
Maybe I should jump
Let myself fall for real

• • •

I'm already doing a good job at watching the mess around
my room tell me I'm clueless about my life

My body hurts
And I don't know what or who or what to hold onto to get
me through
So I listen to sad music
And I cry through the lyrics like I wrote them
Like I was the one who was cheated on
Like I knew that pain

It feels right
To pity myself
To hate my past for grieving my nerves and my legs
For pressuring my back
Scraping on my toes and my feet
So I can't feel them
I'm terrified I won't walk again
I'm terrified I won't get to hold hands at the top of
mountains with my fictional lover
I'm terrified I won't be able to run around with my
fictional children
In my fictional family home with my husband or my wife
I'm delusional about my dreams these days
But this is where I go when I'm feeling my legs scream at
me because basketball won't let me go
It's like an obsessive ex lover
Stalking my every move

Or maybe I won't let that life go
Maybe it's cementing me into a statue of horrors
Reliving the times I had no spine to stand up for myself to
the teammates and coaches that abused me
Forcing me to watch the memories of the past that haunt
me
The ones where I felt invaded
The ones where my space was abused
My heart my spirit my soul my body

• • •

The Crying Man

People Smell:

52

Some people smell like farts
On this bart train
And I'm trying to hold onto the fragrances that I poured
onto my body, my clothes and my hair
But it's so overpowering
The stench of Butt
Circulating the train
In the stains of jeans standing all around me
I wish I didn't have to do this
To sit in a train while people figure out where they should
place their eyes
Invading each other's privacy so easily
So annoyingly

The Woman Called Calm

Tiny Needles:

It's exhausting
Trying to pretend I am fine all day
As soon as 5pm hits I'm a total wreck
I can barely hold my body up
My legs feel like tiny needles are stinging all the way up to
my knees
This terrifies me
I pop one gabapentin
But now I'm not lucid
I feel drunk
Or high
I hate it
I hate it
I hate it
But my legs feel better
And I hate this one more time

Can I go now?

Disability Seat:

People step on my feet every day
They bump into my legs
I'd be madder if I could care more
They're so long I don't blame the people
But I just find it very irritating that
I'm in pain and I can't even catch a break on this disability
seat

Don't Cry in front of Strangers:

There are these moments when I'm in so much pain
That all I can do is stare at the ceiling of the Bart transit
train
And i say to myself I'm praying to god for answers
But in reality, I'm trying hold my eyes open
So, the air of the recycled train can dry the tears ready to
fall
I tell myself I don't cry in front of strangers
When in reality I want to tell myself
I don't cry at all

How Are You?

My coworkers ask me "how are you?"
Sometimes and I say "I am fine"
And I half believe it because I just popped four ibuprofen
and one gabapentin so I lie to myself too

wall.
List of How to Conform
work or Die. or work or Die. or Die. work
Work or Die. work
Door
receptionist
ignoring my existence again
Pretend not to work
TROI
on sale
Sugary Poison
Have a nice day
Chair
Body

Mind Over Matter:

I'm utterly alone inside
In my mind
She tells me I can't handle this
She convinces me everything is pointless
She truly wants to find a way out of this mess
So she pops another pain killer
And tells the world she is okay
Even though she'd be okay if she took too many pills
Maybe that'll help end this suffering
But, mostly she watches people talk about meditation
Wondering if her mind could be the key to getting over
this depressive dedication

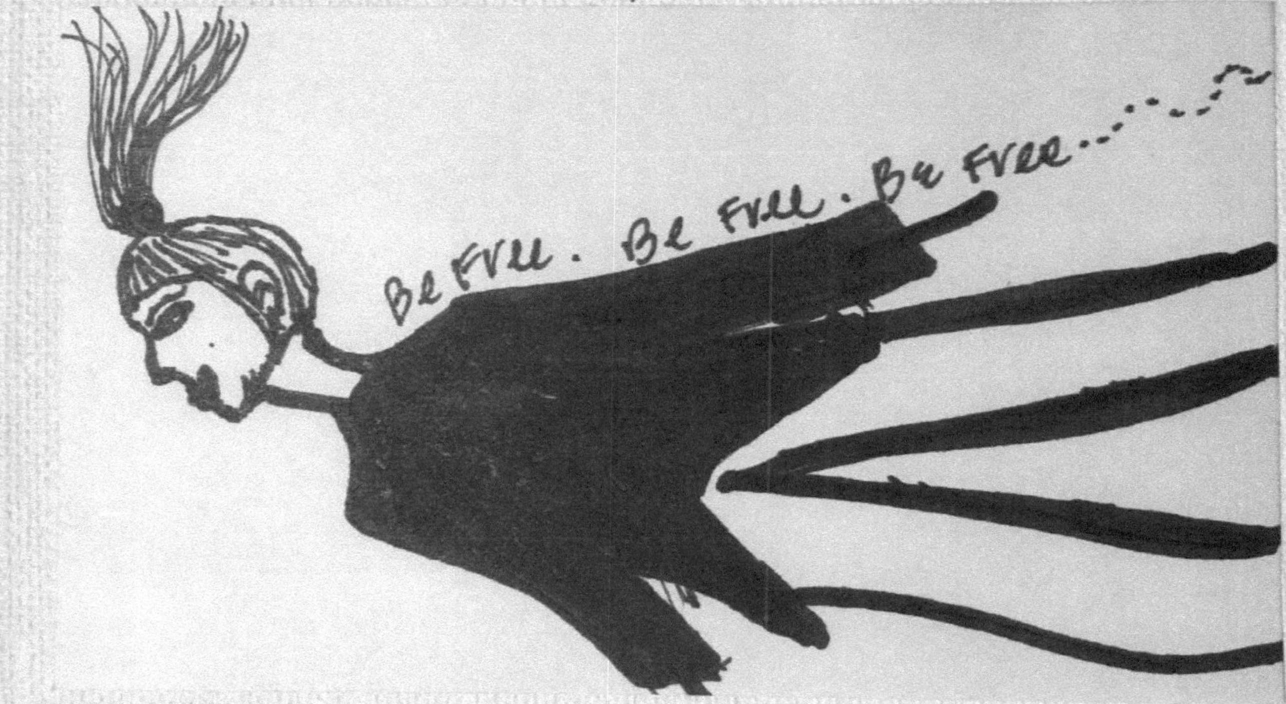

Be free. Be free. Be free......

Facing My Demons:

I let tears fall every time I think about certain people
Alone in my room of course
Or a bathroom
Or my car
Sometimes I hope that the oceans that pour out of my eyes
Can carry me far away from this life
Away from the memories
I wonder when they will stop replaying in my mind
The happy times that are gone
The people I cared about that I can't call
The ones I had to say good-bye to because they never
wanted me
The feelings
I repressed them for so many years
I wonder how many tears are tearing my nerves apart
I wonder if the oceans pouring from my eyes are actually
coming from my bones
Maybe that is why I have so much pain
All those broken memories are stuck inside my spine
Pressuring me to grow up
Face my demons
And glow up

The Tears He Hides

The Crying Man:

I met a man within me
And asked him why he's sad
He told me he needs permission
To say the things that make him mad
I said yes and watched the mystery
Of the man inside my head
Rupturing all of my opinions
In the shapes of good and bad

Mystics in The Forest

Personalities:

She has so many personalities
I like the one where she swears a lot
Swears to god
Swears to the sky
Swears to the apple not being sweet enough
She even swears that her happiness lives deep
inside the ocean
She sits by the beach watching all the people's
madness and commotion
She drinks a bottle of juice mixed with glitter
She calls it her potion

I admire all of the cuss words
They sort of look like running penguins
Jumping in the frozen water
Escaping oz only to be hunted by another demon
Kind of like our positivity
Chased out of town by fear and passivity

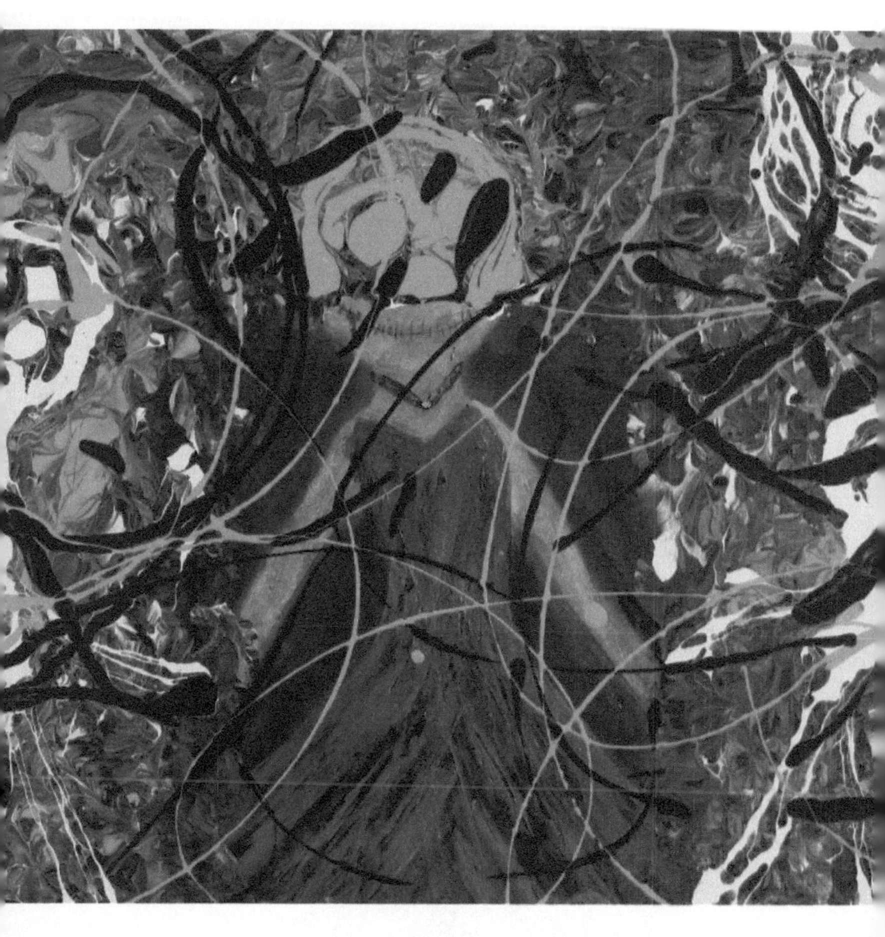

Eve's Hallow

Birds:

I sat at the top of a mountain
And watched 11 falcons
I thought about the tribe they flew with
And wondered where my group was to grow
with
I understood I'm not in wonderland
Because I never met the white rabbit
I feel I am a mad hatter
Stuck in the world of glass
Not shattered

Madness

Fate:

I might never feel good again
That's what I tell myself
So, I don't use pain as an excuse
To hurt people
To be angry at the world
To not fight for my dreams
I tell myself this everyday
Even when I have good days
Because the world will keep going when I feel
weak
People will continue to live when I feel
depressed
People I love may never know how it feels to
live
With a fear of never walking again
Or running again
Or being physically able enough to raise children
And I feel happy for them
I feel happy to see people I love smiling and
laughing
I tell myself I might never feel good again
so, my heart won't be deceived in case they
choose to walk away from me
in case I wake up tomorrow and I am all alone

I won't be surprised when they never call back
I will assume they have gone on to continue to
feel happy and to laugh somewhere else
And I will have lived out my fate

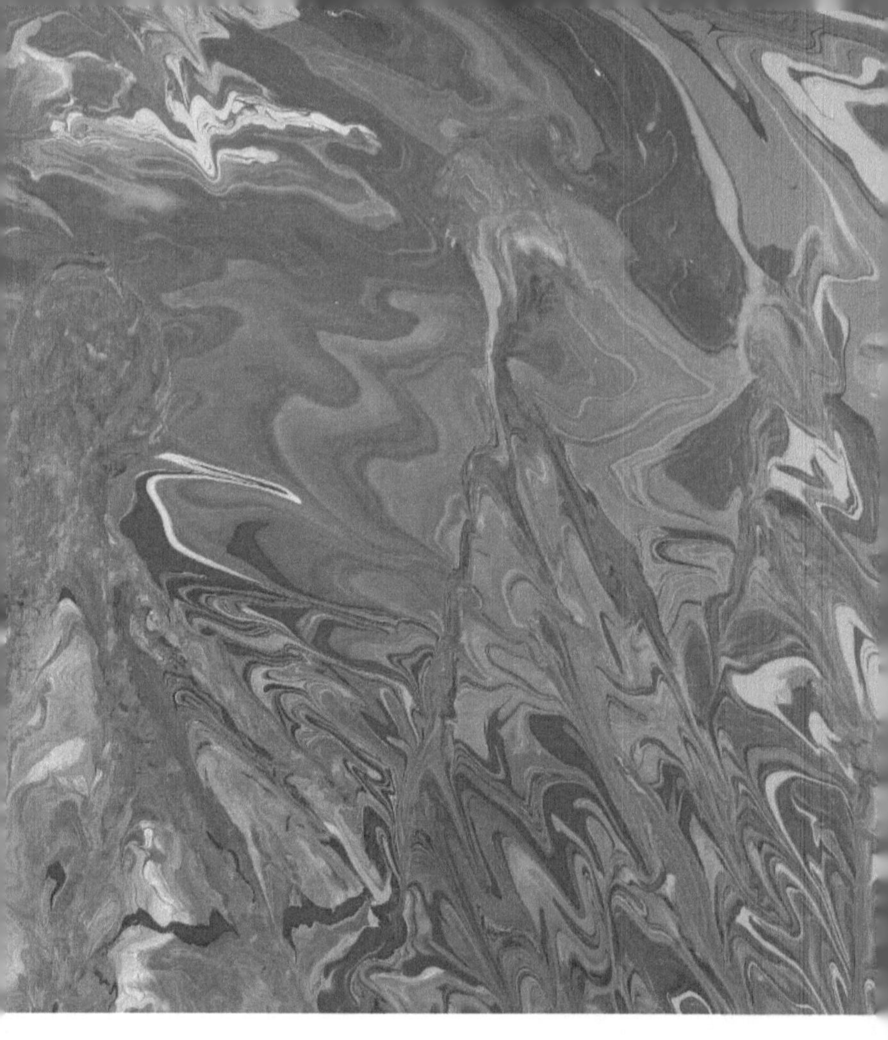

Family Reunions

Puzzle Pieces:

I've fought for years, 10 years to be exact, to get to a place where I could stand up and say what I am saying now. I fought through multiple physical injuries, eating disorders, depression, suicidal thoughts, being hazed in college, being bullied, being excluded by what felt like the world growing up, I fought to do the opposite of the examples I had growing up, I've fought against becoming what my bloodline told me we become, and did I escape oz?

Not quite. I learned that through all this pain, through building my self-worth, self-love and self-confidence that it is an everyday ritual, to decide to believe in myself. It is an everyday health habit to decide consciously if I want to go down that path in my mind, of believing false words placed on my young mind.

I'm saying that after all these years, I realized I don't have to be WHOLE to pursue a happy life. That I just need to keep going, understanding that every broken part of me, can be a puzzle piece to help someone else get through their day a little better. And everyone else who is broken too, you see, we all fit if we stick together. If we don't chip off more of each other because of our pasts.

We're like puzzle pieces to this broken world, that somehow make it whole together. If we decide to

keep going and stay in the present, realizing like we
are perfect in every broken piece and fit into people's
lives when we are meant to, to help them heal and
vice versa. Being broken is a gift. It's in those pieces,
that helps us become the best versions of ourselves.
Those puzzle pieces lay within each of us and in that,
we are all whole together. They are what makes us
human.

The End